Contents

Words in **bold** can be found in the glossary on page 30.

KV-638-746

The world of micro monsters

Curdled milk, furry tomatoes and squirming maggots – these are just some of the signs of food going off. And what's visible to the naked eye isn't the whole story. Many foodstuffs also contain invisible, but deadly, micro monsters!

Tiny living things that you can see only under a microscope are called **microorganisms**. Some of them are micro-animals: insects and other creatures too small to see without a microscope. Other organisms are **microbes**: micro-**fungi**, **bacteria** and **viruses** so tiny that you need super-strong microscopes to see them.

Scanning electron microscopes (SEMs) can magnify things many thousands of times. Let's look at some of the food micro monsters that SEMs can show us.

Using a powerful microscope

Monstrous data

Name	Botulism
Latin name	*Clostridium botulinum*
Adult length	2–22 micrometres
Habitat	Soil, contaminated foods
Lifespan	Its dormant spores can live for years!

Toxic terror

A bacteria called *Clostridium* produces one of nature's deadliest **toxins** – and it sometimes ends up in your food. It usually lives in the soil, but it can survive on vegetables that haven't been canned or **preserved** properly – or even in honey from bees! It's very rare, but if this micro monster finds its way into your body it can cause a serious illness called botulism.

Gross or what?

Signs of botulism include blurred vision, trouble breathing, swallowing and speaking, vomiting, stomach cramps and even paralysis.

A *Clostridium* bacterium magnified 1,025 times

Monstrous habitat

People who can or bottle food at home must follow strict safety guidelines, otherwise the botulism toxin could contaminate the food.

Botulism in children under two is called 'floppy baby syndrome'.

Fifty years ago, half of all patients with botulism died. Today there is better treatment, but it still kills around seven per cent of infected people.

Friendly bacteria

Not all microbes are baddies. Without them, certain foods wouldn't even exist! Take yogurt, for example. It's made from milk by the actions of friendly bacteria, such as *Lactobacillus*.

Friendly bacteria are also known as **probiotics**. Everyone has huge **colonies** of them in their **intestines**. Probiotics help us digest our food and fight off **pathogens** (disease-causing enemy **cells**). We top up our friendly bacteria when we eat foods that contain them, such as yogurt.

Monstrous habitat

Lactobacilli *are what give yogurt its slightly sour taste. Probiotic yogurt contains at least 100 million bacteria cells in every gram!*

Monstrous data

Name	Probiotics
Latin name	*Lactobacillus*
Adult length	1 micrometre
Habitat	Milk products
Lifespan	Constantly dividing and multiplying

Names of bacteria give a clue to their shape. *Bacillus* means rod-shaped, *coccus* means round and *spirilla* means spiral-shaped.

Cartons of drinking yogurt whizz along the production line in a dairy factory.

How yogurt is made

Bacteria are living cells. To **reproduce**, each cell splits itself into two identical 'daughter' cells. It needs energy to do this. *Lactobacillus* bacteria get their energy from lactose, the sugar in milk. They 'feed' on the lactose and create a waste product – their version of poo – called lactic acid, which they excrete (pass out of their cells). Lactic acid makes the **proteins** in the milk stick together more. The result is that the milk changes into thick, creamy yogurt! Yogurt's been made in the same way for thousands of years.

A rod-shaped *Lactobacillus* bacterium, seen through an SEM

Anything that contains the *Lactobacillus* bacteria can start off the **fermenting** process – it could just be a dollop of yogurt.

Gross or what?

In the right conditions, bacteria cells can divide every 20 minutes. That means one mother cell can produce nearly 17 million new bacteria cells in just eight hours!

Cheese worms

Lots of us enjoy a cheese sandwich. Many of us even like eating cheese so old and strong that it smells like stinky feet! But how about cheese with WORMS in it? On the Italian island of Sardinia, it's a speciality!

The cheese is called *casu marzu*, which means 'rotten cheese' – and the worms are actually **larvae**. *Casu marzu* begins life as an ordinary sheep's milk cheese called pecorino, but then the cheese-maker does something a bit weird. He or she leaves the whole cheese outside, with part of the rind cut off to make it easier for cheese flies to get inside and lay their eggs.

Monstrous data

Name	Cheese fly
Latin name	*Piophila casei*
Adult length	4 mm
Habitat	Cheese
Lifespan	20 days

Monstrous habitat

Cheese larvae are encouraged to live in casu marzu. It's not kept in the fridge, because low temperatures would kill the larvae.

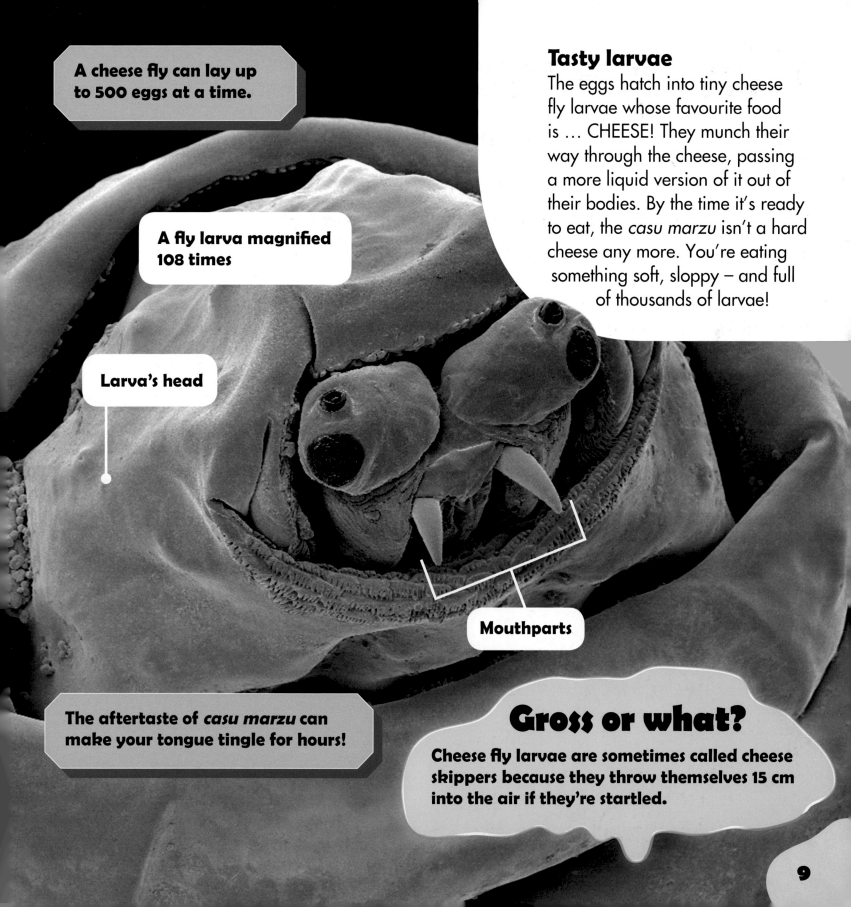

A cheese fly can lay up to 500 eggs at a time.

A fly larva magnified 108 times

Larva's head

Mouthparts

Tasty larvae

The eggs hatch into tiny cheese fly larvae whose favourite food is … CHEESE! They munch their way through the cheese, passing a more liquid version of it out of their bodies. By the time it's ready to eat, the *casu marzu* isn't a hard cheese any more. You're eating something soft, sloppy – and full of thousands of larvae!

The aftertaste of *casu marzu* can make your tongue tingle for hours!

Gross or what?

Cheese fly larvae are sometimes called cheese skippers because they throw themselves 15 cm into the air if they're startled.

Yummy yeast

Yeast belongs to the same family as mushrooms and toadstools – the fungus family. Unlike its larger cousins, a yeast is a micro monster, made up of just one cell.

Yeast may be small, but it does a mighty big job! Without it, we'd miss out on yummy foods such as bread and pizza. That's because when yeast cells feed on sugars, they produce handy by-products, including bubbles of carbon dioxide (this makes bread rise). Alcohol is another by-product – that's why yeast cells are also used to make beer, cider and wine.

Fresh yeast for baking and brewing comes in a 'cake' (above). Most home bakers use granules of dried yeast (below).

Monstrous data

Name	Baker's yeast
Latin name	*Saccharomyces cerevisiae*
Adult length	5–10 micrometres
Habitat	In nature, ripe fruits
Lifespan	2–3 weeks

New cells

Yeast cells usually reproduce by budding – new daughter cells bud off the existing parent cells. The daughter cells are exact copies of the parent cells. Sometimes, though, like other fungi, yeast cells produce clouds of 'seeds' called spores instead.

Daughter cell ready to bud off

Monstrous habitat

When yeast is added to bread dough, it makes the dough rise.

Daughter cell beginning to form

There are 1,500 different species of yeast.

Yeast cells magnified 20,526 times

Yeasts are now being used to make ethanol – an alcohol that can fuel cars!

Evil weevil

You don't need a microscope to see a granary weevil – but it is the best way to get a close-up view of this snouty little insect. Granary weevils don't have many admirers, though – most people view the little critters as HUGE pests!

The clue to the granary weevil's favourite food is in its name. A granary is a place for storing grain, and granary weevils feed on just that. As a result, these micro monsters cause enormous and costly damage each year.

Weevils can easily bore through cardboard boxes or sacking. The safest way to store grain is in metal containers – in a fridge or freezer!

Monstrous data

Name	**Granary weevil**
Latin name	*Sitophilus granarius*
Adult length	4 mm
Habitat	**Grain stores all over the world**
Lifespan	**Up to 8 months as adults**

Monstrous habitat

The granary weevil is sometimes known as the wheat weevil but it feeds on many types of cereal, including oats, rye, barley and corn.

A granary weevil

A threatened weevil will pull in its legs and play dead.

Rice weevils (right) feed on rice, wheat and corn. They are close cousins of granary weevils but they live longer (up to two years) and are able to fly.

Growing up

The female granary weevil lays each of her eggs inside a grain so that when the egg hatches, the plump white larva has a ready supply of food. It goes through its different larval stages and then becomes a **pupa**, all inside the grain. When the adult beetle comes out of its pupa, it uses its long, pointy snout to bore an exit hole through the wall of the hollow grain. Adult weevils give off special chemicals, called pheromones, to attract a mate. After mating, the life cycle begins all over again.

Pantry pest

If you spot stuff that looks like spiders' webs in your food, that's a telltale sign that it might have been infested by Indian meal moth larvae. The webbing is what's left of their cocoons after they pupate.

Indian meal moths are micro monsters that can be a major nuisance all over the world. They lay their eggs on nuts, seeds, cereals, flour, couscous, rice, pasta, dried fruit – pretty much any dry food. The eggs hatch after two to fourteen days, and out come creamy-white larvae with brown heads. These squirming beasties are total eating machines!

Indian meal moth larvae

Monstrous data

Monstrous habitat

Meal moth larvae are found in many different dry foods. Often, the body colour of the larvae matches the colour of the food they eat – perfect camouflage!

Name	Indian meal moth
Latin name	*Plodia interpunctella*
Adult length	8–10 mm
Habitat	Dry foods all over the world
Lifespan	Up to 10 months

A tiny wasp **parasite** lays its eggs inside Indian meal moth larvae – the wasp babies eat the larvae from the inside out!

Adult Indian meal moths only live for a couple of weeks.

Adult Indian meal moths don't feed at all – it's only the larvae that eat.

An adult Indian meal moth on a raisin

From larva to adult

As larvae, Indian meal moths go through up to seven different stages, **moulting** each time to make way for a bigger skin to fit their larger body. In warm temperatures, they go through all their larval stages in about a fortnight. In cooler conditions, it might be nine months before larvae are ready to spin a silken cocoon and pupate. During this time, the larvae grow from being about 0.5 mm long to 12 mm.

Meaty monster

Prepare to meet one of the yuckiest parasites on the planet. This monstrous tapeworm isn't remotely micro in its adult form – but it's pretty small when people first meet it ... in meat!

The pork tapeworm begins life as an egg that is passed out in poo from a human **host**. When eggs or body segments containing eggs are accidentally eaten by pigs or people, they hatch into larvae (called oncospheres). The larvae burrow through the gut wall and into the host's muscles, where they develop into their next life stage – blobby white **cysts**, about a centimetre long.

The ancient Greek scientist Aristotle wrote about pork tapeworms around 2,350 years ago.

Gross or what?

In some parts of Asia, Africa and South America, as many as one in four people are infected by pork tapeworms.

Pork meat that contains tapeworm cysts is called measled pork.

Monstrous data

Name	Pork tapeworm
Latin name	*Taenai solium*
Adult length	Up to 10 m
Habitat	Pigs and people all over the world
Lifespan	Up to 10 months

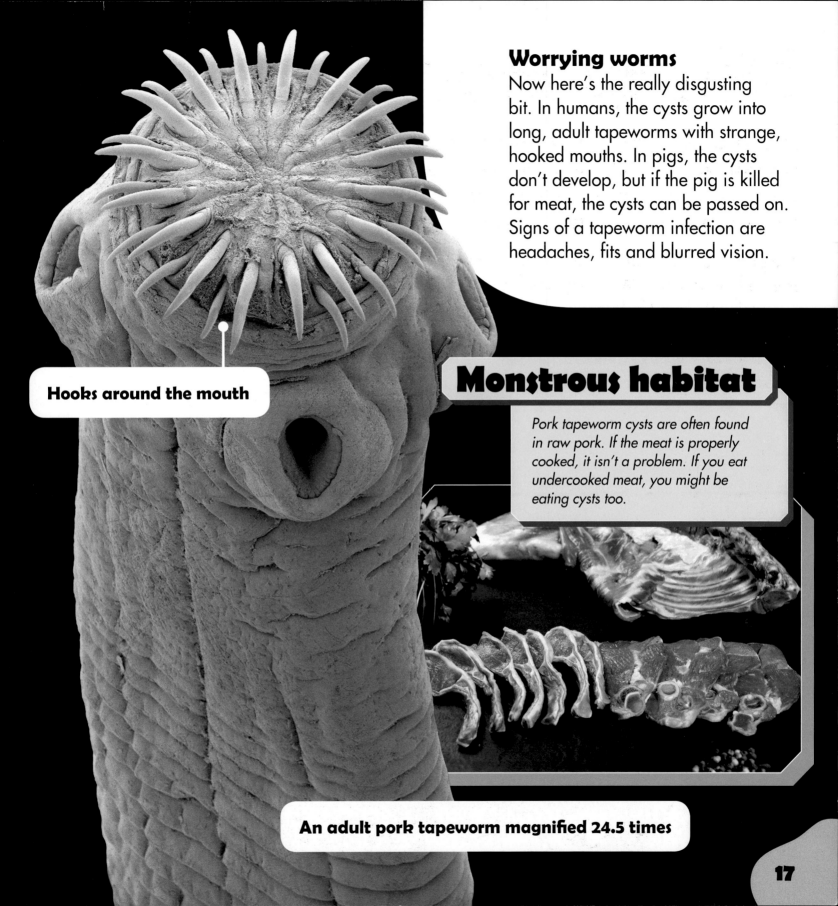

Worrying worms

Now here's the really disgusting bit. In humans, the cysts grow into long, adult tapeworms with strange, hooked mouths. In pigs, the cysts don't develop, but if the pig is killed for meat, the cysts can be passed on. Signs of a tapeworm infection are headaches, fits and blurred vision.

Hooks around the mouth

Monstrous habitat

Pork tapeworm cysts are often found in raw pork. If the meat is properly cooked, it isn't a problem. If you eat undercooked meat, you might be eating cysts too.

An adult pork tapeworm magnified 24.5 times

In from the cold

Most germs are destroyed by low temperatures, but one beastly bacteria isn't at all bothered by the cold. Listeria not only survives in your fridge – it can reproduce in there, too!

Like all bacteria, Listeria are single-celled living things. They reproduce by splitting so that each cell becomes two exact copies of itself. Listeria lives in the soil and, from there, it can get sucked up into grass or other plants and end up in certain foods. If people eat contaminated food, the bacteria enter their gut and then the bloodstream. They become parasites on the body's cells. The result is nasty food poisoning **symptoms** such as diarrhoea, vomiting or – in very rare cases – more serious effects such as swelling of the brain, fits and (for pregnant women) miscarriage.

Monstrous habitat

*Listeria bacteria can lurk in cows' milk. **Pasteurising** the milk kills off any harmful germs with heat.*

Monstrous data

Name	Listeria
Latin name	*Listeria*
Adult length	**500 nanometres**
Habitat	**Soil, animal tissue**
Lifespan	**Constantly dividing and multiplying**

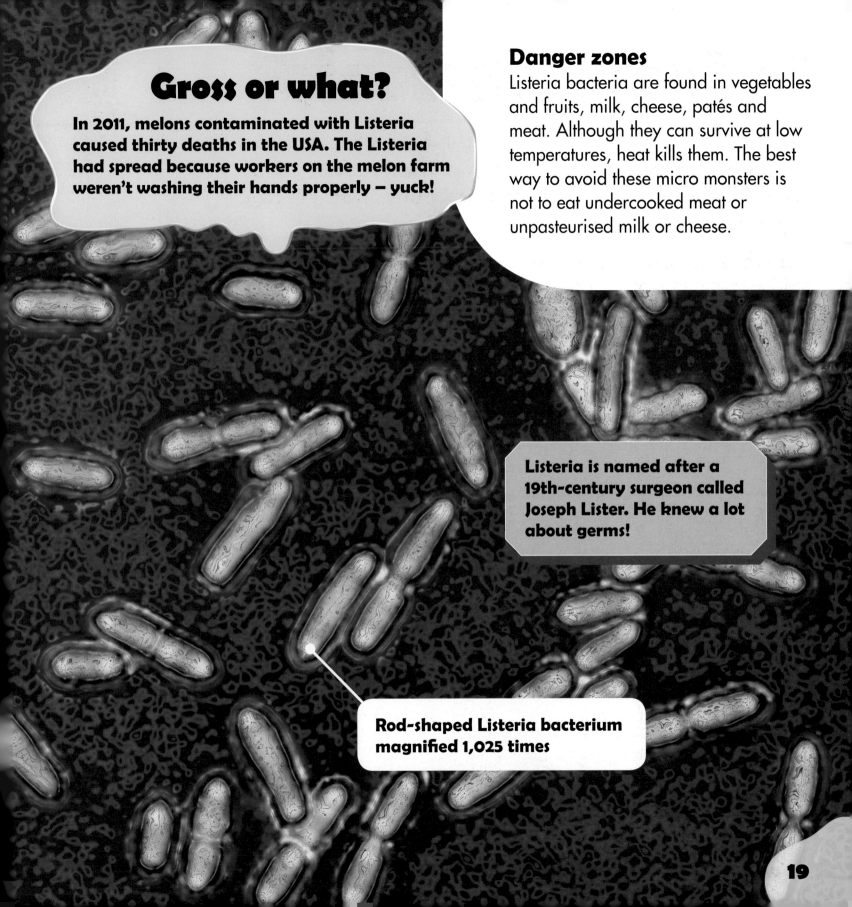

Gross or what?

In 2011, melons contaminated with Listeria caused thirty deaths in the USA. The Listeria had spread because workers on the melon farm weren't washing their hands properly — yuck!

Danger zones

Listeria bacteria are found in vegetables and fruits, milk, cheese, patés and meat. Although they can survive at low temperatures, heat kills them. The best way to avoid these micro monsters is not to eat undercooked meat or unpasteurised milk or cheese.

Listeria is named after a 19th-century surgeon called Joseph Lister. He knew a lot about germs!

Rod-shaped Listeria bacterium magnified 1,025 times

Chicken and egg

Like Listeria, Salmonella is a rod-shaped bacteria that can cause horrible food poisoning. Most people recover after getting Salmonella, but not everyone. In the USA alone, this micro monster causes up to 400 deaths a year.

Salmonella lives in all sorts of animals, both cold- and warm-blooded. One species, *Salmonella enteritidis*, is especially known for infecting poultry, such as chickens, ducks and turkeys, and their eggs. Salmonella can also be passed on by pet snakes and other reptiles.

Eggs from infected hens can contain Salmonella.

Despite its name, Salmonella has nothing to do with salmon fish!

Monstrous data

Name	Salmonella
Latin name	*Salmonella*
Adult length	2–5 micrometres
Habitat	Animals' intestines
Lifespan	Constantly dividing and multiplying

Monstrous habitat

Salmonella is often found in chickens. It doesn't make the birds ill, but it causes sickness if it passes into humans through meat that hasn't been cooked properly.

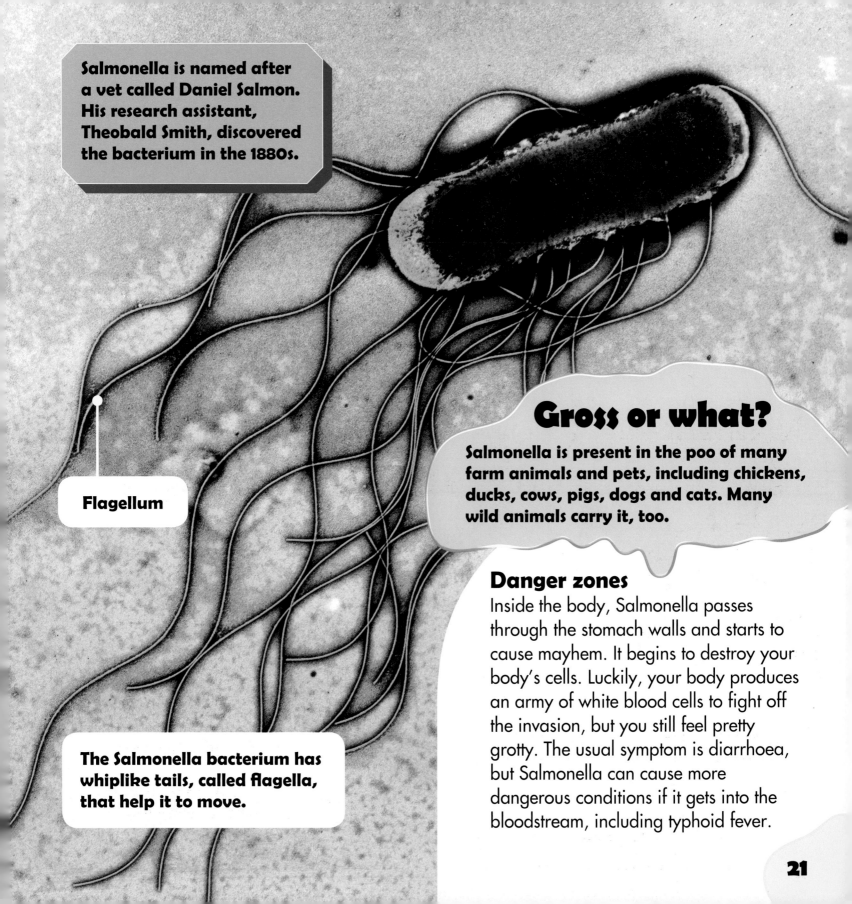

Salmonella is named after a vet called Daniel Salmon. His research assistant, Theobald Smith, discovered the bacterium in the 1880s.

Flagellum

The Salmonella bacterium has whiplike tails, called flagella, that help it to move.

Gross or what?

Salmonella is present in the poo of many farm animals and pets, including chickens, ducks, cows, pigs, dogs and cats. Many wild animals carry it, too.

Danger zones

Inside the body, Salmonella passes through the stomach walls and starts to cause mayhem. It begins to destroy your body's cells. Luckily, your body produces an army of white blood cells to fight off the invasion, but you still feel pretty grotty. The usual symptom is diarrhoea, but Salmonella can cause more dangerous conditions if it gets into the bloodstream, including typhoid fever.

Cheesey cures

Without microbes, cheese wouldn't exist. Most cheeses are produced with the help of bacteria that thicken and flavour the milk. However, some also contain monstrous micro moulds! The mould is what gives blue cheeses their 'veins'.

Cheese-makers use a special technique to make blue cheese – they stick wires or metal rods through the cheese. The holes allow oxygen and mould spores into the cheese. The mould is called *Penicillium*. Traditionally, these cheeses were made in caves where the mould was naturally present. These days, most cheese is made in factories. Instead of leaving nature to do its work, precise amounts of *Penicillium* are stirred into the curds or injected into the cheese.

The furry white 'skin' on a Brie or Camembert cheese is a kind of *Penicillium* mould.

Gross or what?

According to legend, blue cheese was invented by accident. A cheese-maker left his lunch in a cave. A few months later, the bread was mouldy and the mould had spread to the cheese – YUM!

Monstrous data

Name	Mould
Latin name	*Penicillium*
Hyphae length	8 micrometres
Habitat	Dark, damp places – and cheese, of course!
Lifespan	As long as there is moisture and food

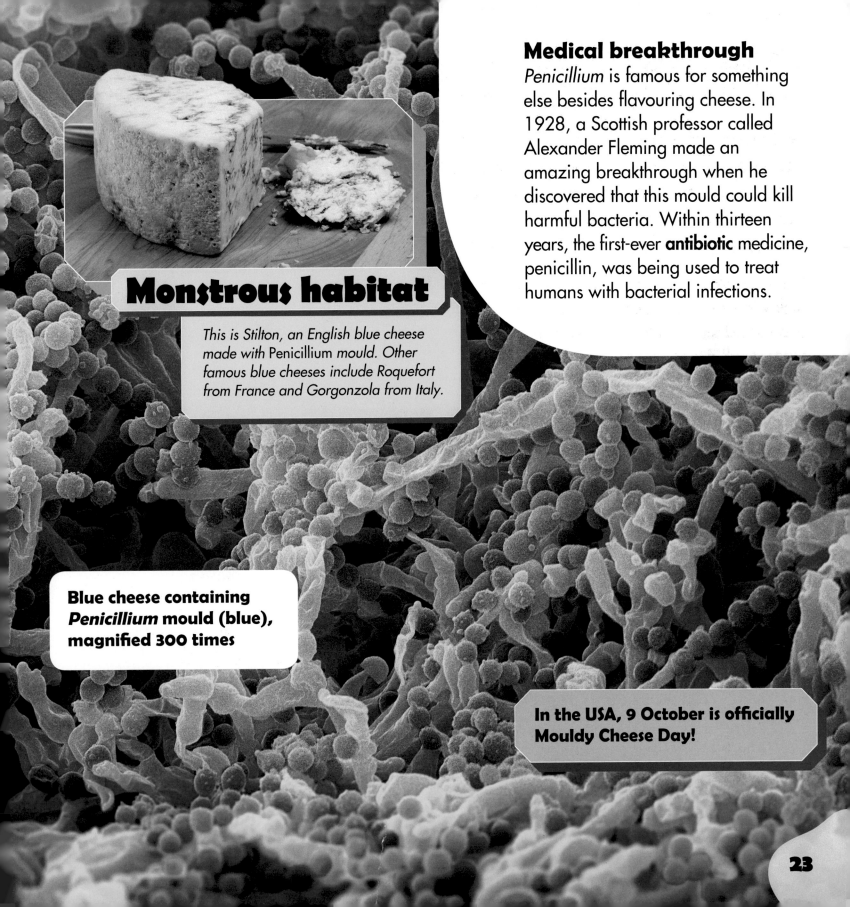

Monstrous habitat

This is Stilton, an English blue cheese made with Penicillium mould. Other famous blue cheeses include Roquefort from France and Gorgonzola from Italy.

Medical breakthrough

Penicillium is famous for something else besides flavouring cheese. In 1928, a Scottish professor called Alexander Fleming made an amazing breakthrough when he discovered that this mould could kill harmful bacteria. Within thirteen years, the first-ever **antibiotic** medicine, penicillin, was being used to treat humans with bacterial infections.

Blue cheese containing *Penicillium* mould (blue), magnified 300 times

In the USA, 9 October is officially Mouldy Cheese Day!

Monstrous mould

Apart from cheese-producers, most people don't want mould anywhere near the food they make or eat! Mould is one of the main microbes that spoil food – the others are yeasts and bacteria.

Spoilt food is any food that's not fit to be eaten – food that tastes 'off', has gone soft and squishy or has furry green stuff growing all over it! When food is really spoilt, the only option is to bin or compost it.

A priest gave the mould Aspergillus its name in 1729 – under the microscope, its shape reminded him of a holy water sprinkler, or *aspergillum*.

Gross or what?

Most of us breathe in Aspergillus spores without a problem, but they can be dangerous for people with allergies or weak lungs.

Monstrous habitat

Aspergillus niger *mould spores are always present in the air. When they land on decaying food, like this squishy tomato, conditions are right for them to grow.*

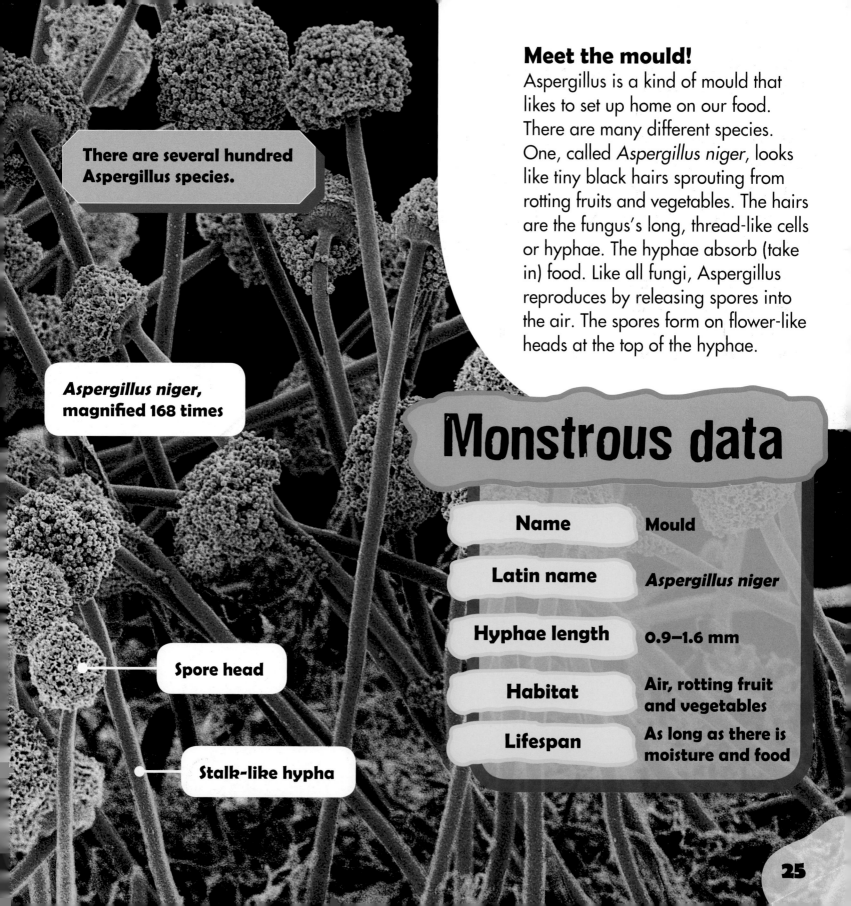

There are several hundred Aspergillus species.

Aspergillus niger,
magnified 168 times

Spore head

Stalk-like hypha

Meet the mould!

Aspergillus is a kind of mould that likes to set up home on our food. There are many different species. One, called *Aspergillus niger*, looks like tiny black hairs sprouting from rotting fruits and vegetables. The hairs are the fungus's long, thread-like cells or hyphae. The hyphae absorb (take in) food. Like all fungi, Aspergillus reproduces by releasing spores into the air. The spores form on flower-like heads at the top of the hyphae.

Monstrous data

Name	Mould
Latin name	*Aspergillus niger*
Hyphae length	0.9–1.6 mm
Habitat	Air, rotting fruit and vegetables
Lifespan	As long as there is moisture and food

Creepy crypto

Cryptos are minute little life forms, or protozoa. They are only made up of one, tiny cell, but they cause massive mayhem if they get into our water or food.

Cryptos start life as spores called oocysts. Thanks to their tough, thick walls, oocysts can stay dormant for years. They are often present in lakes and rivers. If people or animals drink the water, the cryptos can get inside them. Cryptos can also end up on fruit and vegetables and contaminate milk or shellfish.

In 1993, cryptos got into the water supply in Milwaukee, Wisconsin, USA. More than 100 people died, and over 400,000 people were ill with diarrhoea and stomach cramps.

Monstrous data

Name	Crypto
Latin name	*Cryptosporidium*
Oocyst length	4–6 micrometres
Habitat	Freshwater, mammal hosts
Lifespan	In theory, forever!

Monstrous habitat

Crypto spores can sometimes infect drinking water.

The name *Cryptosporidium* means 'secret little spore'.

Inside the host

Once a crypto's been swallowed, the parasite stage of its life begins! The oocyst splits and worm-like life forms wriggle out. These micro monsters feed on the host and go through different life stages until they finally become gamonts – cells that can split to produce new oocysts. These pass out of the host in their poo and enter the sewage system. Then, the cycle then begins all over again.

In this artwork, crypto 'worms' squirm free of their oocyst.

Vegetables can be exposed to cryptos when they're watered. Thoroughly wash any fruit or vegetables that you are going to eat raw. Boiling kills cryptos, too.

Foul flies

You don't need a microscope to see flies buzzing around your food – but it would certainly help you observe all the nasties they spread around. Houseflies carry at least 100 different pathogens!

Blowflies lay their eggs on just-dead corpses. Forensic teams can use fresh and unhatched blowfly eggs to help them determine a time of death.

Houseflies lay their eggs in decaying organic (living or once living) material. They especially like soft or rotting food or poo. The legless little larvae feast for up to two weeks, become a barrel-shaped pupa and then emerge in their adult form with six legs and a pair of wings. Adult flies feed on all sorts of stuff, both yucky and delicious! The bad news is that they spread dangerous microbes, including those that cause diseases such as typhoid fever, cholera and many kinds of food poisoning. Bluebottles, greenbottles and other blowflies can be just as dangerous.

Monstrous habitat

Flies will land on uncovered food. They spread germs with their feet and mouths, and by vomiting or pooing on the food.

Monstrous data

Name	Fruit fly
Latin name	*Drosophila*
Adult length	2–4 mm
Habitat	Decaying fruit
Lifespan	40 days

Fruit flies

A much tinier fly flits around our fruit bowls. Fruit flies don't really spread microbes, but they are still a pest. They speed up the rotting process, and they also attract wasps and other insect hunters.

A fruit fly magnified 150 times

There are nearly 1,500 different species of fruit fly!

The fruit fly's long mouth is shaped like a straw for slurping up decaying fruit.

Glossary

antibiotic a substance that destroys bacteria or stops them growing

bacterium (pl: bacteria) a one-celled organism that is the most numerous living thing in the world. An example is the food-poisoning bug Salmonella

cell the tiny unit that living things are made of

colony a group of the same kind living together

contaminated no longer pure, for example because of containing microbes

cyst a liquid-filled blob. Tapeworms spend part of their life cycle as cysts

dormant sleeping; not active

fermenting changing chemically because of the actions of yeast

fungus (pl: fungi) an organism that lives on and feeds off live or dead organic matter and reproduces with spores. Mushrooms and mildew are both fungi

habitat the place or type of place where an organism usually lives

host an organism that is home to a parasite or a cell that is home to a virus

hypha (pl: hyphae) one of the threads that some fungi use to grow and spread on their host

intestines also called the bowels, the part of the digestive system between the stomach and the anus

larva (pl: larvae) the immature, wingless and wormlike form of an insect that hatches from an egg and later completely changes inside a pupa

microbe any microscopic living thing that is not an animal

micrometre the measurement of length that is one-thousandth of a millimetre and sometimes called a micron

microorganism a living thing too small to see without a microscope

mould a small, furry fungus

moult to shed one's skin

nanometre the measurement of length that is one-millionth of a millimetre and sometimes called a micron

paralysis when a living thing is unable to move

parasite a living thing that lives on or in another living thing and uses its host as food

pasteurise to heat and cool milk in order to kill any microbes

pathogen a microorganism, such as a bacterium, that causes disease

preserved treated to prevent rotting

probiotic describes something that encourages the growth of 'good' microbes

protein one of a group of chemicals that help build body tissue

protozoa a single-celled living thing from the protist kingdom that, like animals, feeds and moves

pupa (pl: pupae) the hard cover that surrounds a larva while it pupates (changes into its adult form)

reproduce produce offspring

species a group of similar organisms that can mate and produce offspring

spore a plant or fungus cell that develops into a new plant or fungus

symptom a sign of a disease or condition

toxin a poison, especially one formed inside the body by microbes

virus a microbe that multiplies by infecting the cells of organisms

Further information

Books

Basher Science: Microbiology
by Dan Green (Kingfisher, 2015)

Build It Yourself: Microbes
by Christine Burillo-Kirch (Nomad Press, 2015)

Complete Book of the Microscope
by Kirsteen Rogers (Usborne, 2012)

Horrible Science: Microscopic Monsters
by Nick Arnold (Scholastic, 2014)

Micro Monsters (Kingfisher, 2010)

Websites

www.childrensuniversity.manchester.ac.uk/learning-activities/science/microorganisms/introduction/
Learn all about microorganisms at the Children's University of the University of Manchester.

commtechlab.msu.edu/sites/dlc-me/zoo/index.html
Visit the Microbe Zoo!

www.sciencephoto.com/dennis-kunkel-microscopy-collection
Some great photos from one of the world's best micro-photographers.

www.microscopy-uk.org.uk/micropolitan/index.html
Wander around the Micropolitan Museum and find 'the smallest page on the web'.

Every effort has been made by the publisher to ensure that these websites contain no inappropriate or offensive material. However, because of the nature of the Internet, it is impossible to guarantee that the content of these sites will not be altered. We strongly advise that Internet access is supervised by a responsible adult.

Measuring the microscopic world

It's hard to imagine how small micrometres and nanometres really are. This picture helps you to see how they compare to a millimetre. Millimetres are pretty tiny themselves, but they are GIANT compared to nanometres. In every millimetre, there are one million nanometres!

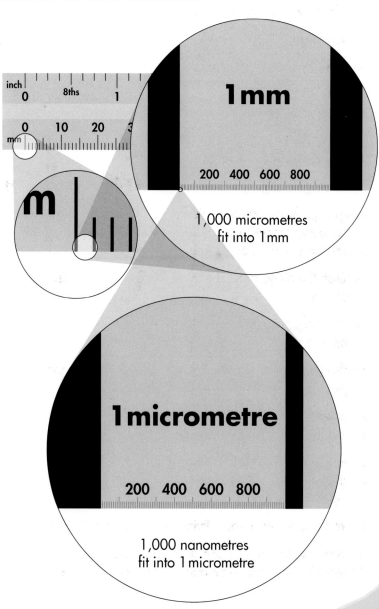

1,000 micrometres fit into 1mm

1,000 nanometres fit into 1 micrometre

Index